Keto Meal Prep

Easy, Healthy and Wholesome Ketogenic Meals to Prep, Grab, and Go
21-day Keto Meal Plan for Beginners

ISBN-13: 978-1726006125
ISBN-10: 1726006123
Brandon Hearn © 2018

Table of Contents

Introduction

Currently, people are constantly on the run. When you're trying to get into a diet, it can be even harder. The ketogenic diet is a great way to lose weight, but it is a diet that is also a lifestyle.

Trying to stick to this lifestyle is difficult without meal prepping, which this book can help you with! Your recipes don't have to be hard to be delicious, and you'll find that there are many recipes in this book that are under an hour to prepare while making multiple servings for days to come.

Just remember that packaging is important when meal prepping, so make sure you have everything you need on hand, and a deep freezer is recommended to keep your food fresh and crisp until you're ready to eat.

The Benefits of Meal Prepping

Meal prepping can help you in a variety of ways, which is what we're going to explore in this chapter. Here are some benefits of meal prepping!

Save Money

You'll save money when you eat healthy and prep in advance. The ketogenic diet can be expensive for people who don't buy in bulk, which is where meal prepping comes in handy.

By planning your meals in advance, you're able to buy in bulk which will save you money. You can usually store a meal for at least two weeks in the freezer too. It can help you save money at lunchtime too when you have prepped leftovers.

Weight Loss

The ketogenic diet already helps you to lose weight but planning your meals in advance will help you to save a little more cash too. With meal planning, you know exactly how much you're going to eat at a time, which can help to keep you from overeating.

A meal routine will also make it easier to know how many net carbs you're putting in your body each day. You can even label the meals with the amount of net carbs in each one.

Easy Grocery Shopping

It's easy to go grocery shopping when you know exactly what you'll be eating and when. Make a list, and just get everything off it. If you are prepping your snacks too, you don't even have to deviate off the list for everything you need.

Just divide your shopping list into different categories like fruits, protein, frozen food, etc., and it'll be easier than ever to avoid aisles where you'd spend too much money or end up straying from the ketogenic diet.

Less Waste

Most of the time, you can just eat out of the dish that you've stored your food in. this helps you to cut down on paper plates, plastic utensils, and will keep you from wasting your food if you've prepped in advance. You unitize all the ingredients that you bought during the week, and it helps you to plan accordingly.

Time Saver

This is the main reason that people decide to start meal prepping. It's hard to find time to cook three meals a day, but that's exactly what the ketogenic diet requires. By saving time when cooking, you're less likely to eat junk food or fast food too.

Stress Reduction

Stress can affect your digestive system, disrupt your sleep and even cause your immune system to suffer. It can be hard to come home from a long day of work and then pan for dinner. With meal prep, you have a dedicated day to get the dinners ready, which allows you to relax most of the time.

How to Start Prepping Today

In this chapter, we'll look at everything you need to start meal prepping today. There are certain ingredients you'll need as well as equipment to get started with.

Meal Prepping Equipment

You'll find essential equipment and what it's used for below.

- **Cutting Board:** You should try to get boards made from solid materials because they're corrosion resistant and non-porous which makes them easier to clean than wood or bamboo boards. Try plastic, glass, or even marble cutting boards for easier clean up.

- **Measuring Cups:** It's important that you measure out your spices and condiments accurately.

- **Measuring Spoons:** Even when you're prepping in bulk, you may still only need a small amount of some spices.

- **Glass Bows:** Glass bowls are considered easier, but nonmetallic containers will also be needed for storing meat and marinades.

- **Packaging Materials:** Your non-metallic containers and glass bowls will be important for this as well, but you may also want bento boxes that are freezer safe or even Tupperware. Make sure that you have freezer safe containers too.

- **Paper Towels & Kitchen Towels:** These will be required for draining meat.

- **Knives:** Your knives should be sharp to slice meat accordingly. Remember to cut away from your body, and you should wash your knives while cutting different food types

- **Kitchen Scale:** A kitchen scale can make some recipes much easier, allowing for much more accurate measurements.

- **Internal Thermometer:** You'll need to check the internal temperature of many meats, especially if you're making snacks like jerky.

- **Baking Sheet:** This will be needed for many recipes, especially sheet cakes, cookies, or even jerky.

- **Colander:** You'll have to drain some vegetables and rices.

- **Skillets & Pans:** It's going to be easier to cook if you have the right sized pan or skillet for what you're doing. You'll need baking dishes too!

Stocking Your Kitchen

While it's impossible to give you a list of each ingredient you'll ever use, there are some basics that you'll want to keep on hand. Before you start prepping for the week, make a comprehensive shopping list according to your meal plan.

- **Cupboard Ingredients:** Sea Salt, Black Pepper, Tomato Sauce, Tomato Paste, Crushed Tomatoes, Garlic Powder, Onion Powder, Ground Spices, Powdered Sweeteners, Liquid Sweeteners, Canned Vegetables, Almond Flour, Coconut Oil, Coconut Milk, Desiccated

Coconut, Nuts & Seeds, Olive Oil, Balsamic Vinegar, White Wine Vinegar.

- **Vegetables:** Avocado, Onions, Fresh Garlic, Zucchini.
- **Fridge:** A Pound of Butter, Cream, Yogurt, Eggs, Baby Carrots, Cherry Tomatoes.

Simple Steps for Meal Prep

For whatever day you get started, you're going to want to streamline the process as much as possible. To do that, just follow the simple steps below to help you get started.

Step 1: Make a Shopping List

You'll want to make a shopping list the day before for best results. In the beginning of your 21-day plan, you'll need to make it for a few short days, but at the end, your shopping list will be for a week at a time. Expect to dedicate most of the day to meal prep but remember that it will make life easier.

Step 2: Go Shopping

You'll want to go in and get out when it comes to the grocery store so that you aren't tempted by unhealthy snacks that will pull you out of ketosis. If you have mostly vegetables, try going to the local farmers market where there's less temptation too. A butcher's shop for your meat can also help.

Step 3: Start with a Clean Area

It's going to be easier to start cooking if you clean your area beforehand, and make sure that you have your containers clean too. It's important to make sure you have everything on hand, and it'll help to make it all go by a little quicker.

Step 4: Start Cooking!

Now the only thing left is to start cooking, but make sure that you let your food completely cool before packing it up. If you don't let your food cool, then you can ruin the texture and it may become soggy upon reheating.

Some Money Saving Tips

Convenience isn't the only reason that you should be meal prepping. Ketogenic meal prepping will help you to save money on what could be an expensive diet if you aren't careful. Here are some tips to help!

Buy in Bulk

If you can, always buy in bulk. A pound of shredded cheese may cost three dollars, but five pounds may cost only six dollars. That's double the price, but you're getting three extra pounds of cheese. The same goes for meat and many other ingredients, including spices. If you're looking for bulk spices, you may want to look for bulk bins at a local whole food store or small markets. Many people can find bulk spices at a farmer's market too.

Look for Sales

You can stock up on things when they're on sale too! Maybe you don't need twenty pounds of chicken that week, but there may be a sale for a buy one gets one free on five-pound bags.

Get at least four and put them in your freezer. You can do this for olive oil, vinegar, and other pantry staples too. This is where a deep freezer comes in handy.

Shop Local

Shopping local can make a large difference too. While stores like Publix or Wal-Mart will have a specific price for vegetables that they have to import to the store, your local farmer's market may make a difference. Local farmers can often offer a lower price on what you're looking for if you're willing to cook based on the season.

21 Day Meal Plan

Meal prepping can be tricky to get started with because you don't want to cook for the first week, but this isn't a possibility.

The goal with meal prepping is to slowly cut down on how many times you must cook in a week down to only one day per week, and to do that you need to build up your freezer.

For the first time, it's good to only must cook every other day, and then move to every three days, then every four days, and then you should have enough in your freezer to make it every week.

Here's a 21-day meal plan that will help you to start meal prepping properly. Just remember to label all your food with the day that you made it as well as the net carbs. This will let you know exactly how many net carbs you're putting into your body, helping you to stay on the ketogenic diet. It also helps you to slowly rotate the food you have in your freezer to avoid frostbite or spoiling.

Day 1

Breakfast: Berry Smoothie
- **Net Carbs:** 8

Lunch: BLT Salad
- **Net Carbs:** 2

Snack: Green Salmon Bites
- **Net Carbs:** 5

Dinner: Ginger Soup
- **Net Carbs:** 5

Dessert: Coconut Macaroons
- **Net Carbs:** 2

Daily Net Carbs: 22

Day 2

Breakfast: Yogurt Parfait
- **Net Carbs:** 9

Lunch: BLT Salad
- **Net Carbs:** 2

Snack: Spinach Dip
- **Net Carbs:** 4

Dinner: Buttery Garlic Shrimp
- **Net Carbs:** 4
- **Side Dish:** Creamed Spinach
  - **Net Carbs:** 1

Dessert: Chocolate Bacon
- **Net Carbs:** 0.5

Daily Net Carbs: 20.5

Day 3

Breakfast: Yogurt Parfait
- **Net Carbs:** 9

Lunch: Fish Curry
- **Net Carbs:** 4

Snack: Green Salmon Bites
- **Net Carbs:** 5

Dinner: Ginger Soup
- **Net Carbs:** 5

Dessert: Banana Fat Bombs
- **Net Carbs:** 1

Daily Net Carbs: 24

Day 4

Breakfast: Green Smoothie
- **Net Carbs:** 9

Lunch: BLT Salad
- **Net Carbs:** 2

Snack: Cheesy Bacon Deviled Eggs
- **Net Carbs:** 2

Dinner: Herb Pork Chops
- **Net Carbs:** 0
- **Side Dish:** Creamed Spinach
    - **Net Carbs:** 1

Dessert: Raspberry Popsicle
- **Net Carbs:** 8

Daily Net Carbs: 22

Day 5

Breakfast: Yogurt Parfait
- **Net Carbs:** 9

Lunch: Twisted Tuna Salad
- **Net Carbs:** 5

Snack: Cheesy Bacon Deviled Eggs
- **Net Carbs:** 2

Dinner: Buttery Garlic Shrimp
- **Net Carbs:** 4
- **Side Dish:** Roasted Radishes
  - **Net Carbs:** 2

Dessert: Vanilla Pudding
- **Net Carbs:** 2

Daily Net Carbs: 24

Day 6

Breakfast: Cinnamon Smoothie
- **Net Carbs:** 6

Lunch: Half Hour Chili
- **Net Carbs:** 5

Snack: Walnut Crusted Goat Cheese
- **Net Carbs:** 2

Dinner: Taco Casserole
- **Net Carbs:** 4

Dessert: Coconut Macaroons
- **Net Carbs:** 2

Daily Net Carbs: 19

Day 7

Breakfast: Green Smoothie
- **Net Carbs:** 9

Lunch: Crab Stuffed Avocado
- **Net Carbs:** 5

Snack: Green Salmon Bites
- **Net Carbs:** 5

Dinner: Beef Cabbage Rolls
- **Net Carbs:** 4

Dessert: Vanilla Pudding
- **Net Carbs:** 2

Daily Net Carbs: 25

Day 8

Breakfast: Cinnamon Smoothie
- **Net Carbs:** 6

Lunch: Fish Curry
- **Net Carbs:** 4

Snack: Walnut Crusted Goat Cheese
- **Net Carbs:** 2

Dinner: Ginger Soup
- **Net Carbs:** 5

Dessert: Raspberry Popsicle
- **Net Carbs:** 8

Daily Net Carbs: 25

Day 9

Breakfast: Yogurt Parfait
- **Net Carbs:** 9

Lunch: Crab Stuffed Avocado
- **Net Carbs:** 5

Snack: Green Salmon Bites
- **Net Carbs:** 5

Dinner: Beef Cabbage Rolls
- **Net Carbs:** 4

Dessert: Chocolate Bacon
- **Net Carbs:** 0.5

Daily Net Carbs: 24.5

Day 10

Breakfast: Coconut & Cinnamon Porridge
- **Net Carbs:** 6

Lunch: BLT Salad
- **Net Carbs:** 2

Snack: Pepper & Bacon Bombs
- **Net Carbs:** 0

Dinner: Taco Casserole
- **Net Carbs:** 4

Dessert: Poppy Seed Cupcakes
- **Net Carbs:** 14

Daily Net Carbs: 26

Day 11

Breakfast: Green Smoothie
- **Net Carbs:** 9

Lunch: Fish Curry
- **Net Carbs:** 4

Snack: Green Salmon Bites
- **Net Carbs:** 5

Dinner: Ginger Soup
- **Net Carbs:** 5 Grams

Dessert: Chocolate Bacon
- **Net Carbs:** 0.5 Grams

Daily Net Carbs: 23

Day 12

Breakfast: Cinnamon & Coconut Porridge
- **Net Carbs:** 6

Lunch: Half Hour Chili
- **Net Carbs:** 5

Snack: Pepper & Bacon Bombs
- **Net Carbs:** 0

Dinner: Taco Casserole
- **Net Carbs:** 4

Dessert: Raspberry Popsicles
- **Net Carbs:** 8

Daily Net Carbs: 23

Day 13

Breakfast: Egg & Bacon Cups
- **Net Carbs:** 1

Lunch: Fish Curry
- **Net Carbs:** 4

Snack: Chocolate Bacon
- **Net Carbs:** 0.5

Dinner: Beef Cabbage Rolls
- **Net Carbs:** 4

Desert: Poppy Seed Cupcakes
- **Net Carbs:** 14

Daily Net Carbs: 23.5

Day 14

Breakfast: Cinnamon & Coconut Porridge
- **Net Carbs:** 6

Lunch: Half Hour Chili
- **Net Carbs:** 5

Snack: Pepper & Bacon Bombs
- **Net Carbs:** 0

Dinner: Coconut Chicken
- **Net Carbs:** 4
- **Side Dish:** Parmesan Pork Green Beans
  - **Net Carbs:** 5

Dessert: Chocolate Bacon
- **Net Carbs:** 0.5

Daily Net Carbs: 20.5

Day 15

Breakfast: Egg & Bacon Cup
- **Net Carbs:** 1

Lunch: Arugula Shrimp Salad
- **Net Carbs:** 4

Snack: Walnut Crusted Goat Cheese
- **Net Carbs:** 2

Dinner: Herb Pork Chops
- **Net Carbs:** 0
- **Side Dish:** Roasted Radishes
  - **Net Carbs: 2**

Dessert: Poppy Seed Cupcakes
- **Net Carbs:** 14

Daily Net Carbs: 23

Day 16

Breakfast: Cinnamon Smoothie
- **Net Carbs:** 6

Lunch: Arugula Shrimp Salad
- **Net Carbs:** 4

Snack: Pepper & Bacon Bombs
- **Net Carbs:** 0

Dinner: Steak & Broccoli Medley
- **Net Carbs:** 10

Dessert: Banana Fat Bomb
- **Net Carbs:** 1

Daily Net Carbs: 21

Day 17

Breakfast: Egg & Bacon Cups
- **Net Carbs:** 1

Lunch: Half Hour Chili
- **Net Carbs:** 5

Snack: Walnut Crusted Goat Cheese
- **Net Carbs:** 2

Dinner: Beef Cabbage Rolls
- **Net Carbs:** 4

Dessert: Raspberry Popsicles
- **Net Carbs:** 8

Daily Net Carbs: 20

Day 18

Breakfast: Cinnamon & Coconut Porridge
- **Net Carbs:** 6

Lunch: Arugula Shrimp Salad
- **Net Carbs:** 4

Snack: Pepper & Bacon Fat Bombs
- **Net Carbs:** 0

Dinner: Steak & Broccoli Medley
- **Net Carbs:** 10

Dessert: Banana Fat Bombs
- **Net Carbs:** 1

Daily Net Carbs: 21

Day 19

Breakfast: Berry Smoothie
- **Net Carbs:** 8

Lunch: Twisted Tuna Salad
- **Net Carbs:** 5

Snack: Spinach Dip
- **Net Carbs:** 4

Dinner: Grilled Chicken & Cheesy Spinach
- **Net Carbs:** 3

Dessert: Chocolate Bacon
- **Net Carbs:** 0.5

Daily Net Carbs: 20.5

Day 20

Breakfast: Egg & Bacon Cups
- **Net Carbs:** 1

Lunch: Arugula Shrimp Salad
- **Net Carbs:** 4

Snack: Walnut Crusted Goat Cheese
- **Net Carbs:** 2

Dinner: Herb Pork Chops
- **Net Carbs:** 0
- **Side Dish:** Garlic Artichokes
  - **Net Carbs:** 12

Dessert: Banana Fat Bombs
- **Net Carbs:** 1

Daily Net Carbs: 20

Day 21

Breakfast: Cinnamon Smoothie
- **Net Carbs:** 6

Lunch: Twisted Tuna Salad
- **Net Carbs:** 5

Snack: Spinach Dip
- **Net Carbs:** 4

Dinner: Grilled Chicken & Cheesy Spinach
- **Net Carbs:** 3

Desert: Vanilla Pudding
- **Net Carbs:** 2

Daily Net Carbs: 20

A Reminder

As you continue to plan your meals throughout the three weeks, you'll notice that you have more and more of your meals in the freezer. The first two days you'll likely be cooking, and that will give you leftovers, and then you can slowly start skipping more and more days. Just remember that if you keep your meal planning up, you'll soon be able to dedicate only one day per week to cooking, which most people take Sunday as their meal-prepping day.

Breakfast Recipes

Here are some breakfast recipes to get you started!

Egg & Bacon Cups

Serves: 6 **Time:** 25 Minutes
Calories: 101 **Fat:** 7 Grams
Protein: 8 Grams **Net Carbs:** 1 Gram
Ingredients:

- 6 Bacon Strips
- 6 Eggs, Large
- ¼ Cup Cheddar Cheese, Shredded
- Handful of Spinach, Fresh
- Sea Salt & Black Pepper to Taste

Directions:

1. Start by heating your oven to 400.
2. Fry the bacon in a skillet using medium heat, and then drain the oil, placing it to the side.
3. Grease your muffin tin with the bacon grease, lining each one with a slice of bacon.
4. Beat your eggs in a bowl.
5. Add your spinach to the egg mixture, and then divide it between your muffin tins.
6. Sprinkle with cheese and season, baking for another fifteen minutes.

Yogurt Parfait

Serves: 4
Time: 10 Minutes
Calories: 230 **Protein:** 20 Grams
Fat: 15 Grams **Net Carbs:** 9 Grams
Ingredients:

- 1 Cup Flax Seeds Toasted
- 1 Cup Macadamia, Pieces
- 1 Cup Walnuts ,Toasted
- 1 Cup Coconut, Shredded
- Sweetener to Taste
- 2 Cups Yogurt, Full Fat
- 4 Handful Blueberries
- 4 Bananas, Sliced
- 4 Handfuls Strawberries

Directions:

1. Add three tablespoons of yogurt to the bottom of the jars, adding in your sweetener. Layer with nuts, coconuts, and fruit alternately between ingredients, topping with remaining yogurt.

Coconut & Cinnamon Porridge

Serves: 4
Time: 10 Minutes
Calories: 171 **Protein:** 2 Grams
Fat: 16 Grams **Net Carbs:** 6 Grams
Ingredients:

- 2 Cups Water
- ½ Cup Coconut, Shredded & Unsweetened
- 1 Cup Heavy Cream
- 2 Tablespoons Oat Bran
- 1 Tablespoon Butter
- 2 Tablespoons Flaxseed Meal
- 1 ½ Teaspoons Stevia
- 1 Teaspoon Cinnamon
- Sea Salt to Taste
- Blueberries to Garnish

Directions:

1. Mix all ingredients in a pot, bringing to a slow boil over medium-low heat.
2. Stir and remove from heat, allowing it to sit for ten minutes before topping to serve.

Artichoke & Bacon Omelet

Serves: 4 **Time:** 20 Minutes
Calories: 435 **Protein:** 17 Grams
Fat: 39 Grams **Net Carbs:** 3
Ingredients:

- 6 Eggs, Beaten
- 1 Tablespoon Olive Oil
- 2 Tablespoons Heavy Whipping Cream
- 8 Bacon Slices, cooked 7 Chopped
- ¼ Cup Onion, Chopped
- ½ Cup Artichoke Hearts, Chopped
- Sea Salt & Black Pepper to Taste

Directions:

1. Whisk your heavy cream, eggs, and bacon together until blended well.
2. Put a skillet over medium-high heat, adding in your olive oil.
3. Sauté your onion until it's tender, which should take three minutes.
4. Pour the egg mixture into your skillet, swirling it and allowing it to cook for a full minute.
5. Lift the edges up so that the uncooked egg flows to the underside, and allow it to cook for two more minutes.
6. Sprinkle on your artichoke hearts before flipping your omelet, cooking for another four minutes. Your egg should be firm and then flip the omelet again.
7. Remove from heat, and then season before serving.

Cinnamon Smoothie

Serves: 4
Time: 10 Minutes
Calories: 492 **Protein:** 18 Grams
Fat: 47 Grams **Net Carbs:** 6 Grams
Ingredients:

- 4 Cups Coconut Milk
- 10 Drops Liquid Stevia
- 2 Scoops Vanilla Protein Powder
- 1 Teaspoon Vanilla Extract
- 2 Teaspoons Cinnamon

Directions:

1. Blend everything together until smooth.

Blueberry & Spinach Smoothie

Serves: 4
Time: 5 Minutes
Calories: 353 **Protein:** 15 Grams
Fat: 32 Grams **Net Carbs:** 6 Grams
Ingredients:

- 1 English Cucumber
- 2 Cups Coconut Milk
- 2 Cups Spinach
- 1 Cup Blueberries
- 2 Scoops Protein Powder, Plain
- 4 Tablespoons Coconut Oil
- 8 Ice Cubes
- Mint Sprigs to Garnish

Directions:

1. Blend everything together until smooth, serving with mint sprigs to garnish.

Berry Smoothie

Serves: 1
Time: 5 Minutes
Calories: 221
Protein: 21 Grams
Fat: 9 Grams
Net Carbs: 8 Grams
Ingredients:

- ¼ Cup Blueberries, Frozen
- ¼ Cup Blackberries, Frozen
- 3 Teaspoons Flaxseed
- 1 Teaspoon Vanilla Bean Extract
- 1 Cup Almond Milk, Unsweetened
- 1 Scoop Greek Yogurt, Chilled
- Stevia as Desired

Directions:

1. Blend everything until smooth and serve immediately.

Cheese & Ham Waffles

Serves: 2 **Time:** 15 Minutes
Calories: 620
Protein: 45 Grams **Fat:** 50 Grams **Net Carbs:** 1 Gram

Ingredients:
- 8 Eggs
- 1 Teaspoon Baking Powder
- 2 Ounces Cheddar Cheese, Grated
- Basil to Taste
- Paprika to Taste
- 2 Ounces Ham Steak, Chopped
- 1 Teaspoon Sea Salt, Fine
- 12 Tablespoons Butter, Melted

Directions:
1. Crack four eggs in two bowls, separating your yolks and whites.
2. Add your baking powder, salt and butter, whisking.
3. Fold your ham into your yolk.
4. Mix your egg whites with salt, whisking until stiff peaks form.
5. Fold half of your egg whites into the yolk mixture, allowing it to settle for a few minutes.
6. Fold in the remaining egg whites, and then cook your waffles for four minutes each. Repeat until all your batter is used.

Green Smoothie

Serves: 3
Time: 10 Minutes
Calories: 218
Protein: 3 Grams
Fat: 21 Grams
Net Carbs: 9 Grams
Ingredients:
- ½ Avocado, Peeled & Pitted
- 7 Ounces Coconut Milk, Unsweetened & Full Fat
- ½ Cup Cucumber, Diced
- 1 Cup Baby Kale, Chopped
- 2 Tablespoons Lemon Juice, Fresh
- 2 Tablespoons Orange Juice, Fresh
- Water as Needed

Directions:
1. Blend all ingredients together and serve immediately.

Lunch Recipes

Lunch is an important meal of the day, but it can be a time when people are very busy. Luckily, with planned and prepped meals, it's a little easier to eat healthy lunches.

BLT Salad

Serves: 4
Time: 15 Minutes
Calories: 228
Protein: 1 Gram
Fat: 18 Grams
Net Carbs: 2 Grams
Ingredients:

- 2 Tablespoons Bacon Fat, Melted
- 2 Tablespoon Red Wine Vinegar
- 4 Cups Lettuce Shredded
- Black Pepper to Taste

- 1 Tomato, Chopped
- 2 Hardboiled Eggs, Chopped
- 6 Bacon Slices, Cooked & Chopped
- 1 Tablespoon Roasted Sunflower Seeds, Unsalted
- 1 Chicken Breast, Cooked & Sliced
- 1 Teaspoon Sesame Seeds, Toasted

Directions:
1. Whisk your bacon fat and vinegar together until it emulsifies. Season with pepper.
2. Toss your vegetables, tomato and lettuce in a bowl with your dressing.
3. Divide between plates and top with bacon, egg, sunflower seeds, sesame seeds and chicken before serving.

Fish Curry

Serves: 4 **Time:** 35 Minutes
Calories: 416
Protein: 26 Grams **Fat:** 31 Grams **Net Carbs:** 4 Grams
Ingredients:

- 2 Tablespoons Coconut Oil
- 2 Teaspoons Garlic Minced
- 1 ½ Tablespoons Ginger, Grated Fresh
- 1 Tablespoon Curry Powder
- ½ Teaspoon Ground Cumin
- 2 Cups Coconut Milk
- 16 Ounces White Fish, Chopped into 1 Inch Chunks
- 1 Cup Kale, Shredded
- 2 Tablespoons Cilantro, Chopped

Directions:

1. Put a saucepan over medium heat, melting your coconut oil. Sauté your garlic and ginger until lightly browned, which should take about two minutes.

2. Stir your curry and cumin in, sautéing until it's fragrant. This should take about two minutes. Stir in your coconut milk, allowing it to come to a boil.

3. Reduce your heat to low, simmering for five minutes.

4. Add your fish, cooking for ten minutes.

5. Stir in your cilantro and kale, simmering until it's wilted. This should take two minutes and serve warm.

Avocado & Chicken Wraps

Serves: 4
Time: 10 Minutes
Calories: 264 **Protein:** 12 Grams
Fat: 20 Grams **Net Carbs:** 6 Grams
Ingredients:

- ½ Avocado, Peeled & Pitted
- 2 Teaspoons Thyme Fresh & Chopped
- 1/3 Cup Creamy Mayonnaise
- 1 Teaspoon Lemon Juice, Squeezed Fresh
- 6 Ounces Chicken Breasts Cooked & Chopped
- 8 Lettuce Leaves, Large
- Black Pepper to Taste
- ¼ Cup Walnuts, Chopped

Directions:

1. Mash the avocado in a bowl, adding your lemon juice, thyme and mayonnaise. Mix well.
2. Stir in your chicken, seasoning with salt and pepper.
3. Spoon your mixture into the lettuce leaves, topping with walnuts before wrapping to serve.

Turkey Wraps

Serves: 6 **Time:** 20 Minutes
Calories: 162 **Protein:** 23 Grams
Fat: 4 Grams **Net Carbs:** 7 Grams
Ingredients:

- 1 ¼ lbs. Ground Turkey, Lean
- 4 Green Onions, Minced
- 1 Tablespoon Olive Oil
- 1 Clove Garlic, Minced
- 8 Ounces Water Chestnut, Diced
- 2 Teaspoons Chili Paste
- 3 Tablespoons Hoisin Sauce
- 2 Tablespoons Coconut Aminos
- 12 Butter Lettuce Leaves
- 1 Tablespoon Rice Vinegar
- Sea Salt to Taste

Directions:

1. Place your pan over medium heat, adding in garlic and turkey.
2. Heat for six minutes. Your turkey should be well cooked, and then transfer it in a bowl. Add in your onion and water chestnuts, stirring.
3. Stir in your coconut aminos, hoisin sauce, chili paste and vinegar.
4. Divide between lettuce leaves.

Half Hour Chili

Serves: 6 **Time:** 40 Minutes
Calories: 400 **Protein:** 31 Grams
Fat: 27 Grams **Net Carbs:** 5 Grams
Ingredients:

- 2 lbs. Ground Beef
- 8 Ounces Spinach
- 1 Cup Tomato Sauce, Low Carb
- 2 Green Bell Peppers
- ¼ Cup Parmesan Cheese
- 2/3 Onion, Chopped
- 2 Teaspoons Cayenne Pepper
- 1 ½ Tablespoons Chili Powder
- 1 Tablespoon Cumin
- 1 Tablespoon Olive Oil
- 1 Teaspoon Garlic Powder/ Sea Salt & Black Pepper to Taste

Directions:

1. Dice your bell pepper and onion, sautéing over medium heat with olive oil, seasoning with salt and pepper. Stir while cooking.

2. Put a pot over medium heat, adding in your ground beef, seasoning with salt and pepper. Season with spices, and then reduce heat.

3. Once your beef is browned, add your spinach, and allow it to steam for three minutes. Stir into the beef, and then add in your tomato sauce stirring again. Reduce heat to medium-low cooking for ten minutes.

4. Add in your sautéed vegetables and cheese, stirring together. Allow to cook for a few more minutes before serving.

Arugula Shrimp Salad

Serves: 8
Time: 10 Minutes
Calories: 328
Protein: 6 Grams
Fat: 24 Grams
Net Carbs: 4 Grams
Ingredients:
- 16 Cups Arugula
- 2 lbs. Shrimp, Cooked & Peeled
- 8 Tablespoon Olive Oil
- 4 Lemons, 2 Juiced & 2 Cut to Serve
- 2 Avocados, Diced
- Sea Salt & Black Pepper to Taste

Directions:
1. Add your olive oil, lemon juice sea salt and pepper together to make your dressing.
2. Mix your shrimp, arugula and avocado together.
3. Drizzle with your dressing and serve with lemon wedges.

Crab Stuffed Avocados

Serves: 2
Time: 20 Minutes
Calories: 389
Protein: 19 Grams
Fat: 31 Grams
Net Carbs: 5 Grams
Ingredients:

- 1 Avocado, Peeled, Halved & Pitted
- 4 ½ Ounces Dungeness Crabmeat
- ½ Teaspoon Lemon Juice, Fresh
- ¼ Cup English Cucumber, Chopped & Peeled
- ½ Cup Cream Cheese
- ¼ Cup Red Bell Pepper, Chopped
- ½ Scallion, Chopped
- 1 Teaspoon Cilantro, Chopped
- Sea Salt & Black Pepper to Taste

Directions:

1. Brush the cuts on the avocado with lemon juice before setting them on a plate.
2. In a bowl, mix all your ingredients together.
3. Divide it between the avocados before serving.

Twisted Tuna Salad

Serves: 6
Time: 15 Minutes
Calories: 352
Protein: 25 Grams
Fat: 26 Grams
Net Carbs: 5 Grams
Ingredients:

- 10 Ounces Endive Leaves, Separated
- 15 Ounces White Albacore Tuna in Oil, Solid & Drained
- 1 ½ Cups Feta Cheese, Crumbled
- ¾ Cup Olive Oil
- ¾ Cup Roasted Red Pepper, Diced
- 1 ½ Tablespoons Capers, Drained
- 1/3 Cup Green Olives, Quartered
- 1/3 Cup Parsley, Fresh & Chopped
- 1 ½ Tablespoons Lemon Juice
- Red Pepper Flakes to Taste
- Sea Salt & Black Pepper to Taste

Directions:

1. Crumble your tuna in a bowl, mixing all your ingredients together before serving.

Snack Recipes

On any diet, you're going to get hungry from time to time, and that's where these snack recipes come in handy. They're also perfect to bring to a party.

Smoked Salmon Fat Bombs

Serves: 12 (6 Servings)
Time: 2 Hours 10 Minutes
Calories: 193
Protein: 8 Grams **Fat:** 18 Grams **Net Carbs:** 0 Grams
Ingredients:
- ½ Cup Goat Cheese, Room Temperature
- 2 Ounces Smoked Salmon
- ½ Cup Butter, Room Temperature
- 2 Teaspoons Lemon Juice, Fresh
- Black Pepper to Taste

Directions:
1. Start by lining a baking sheet using parchment paper.
2. Get out a bowl, mixing your goat cheese, smoked salmon, butter, lemon juice and pepper together. Make sure it's blended well.
3. Use a tablespoon to scoop the mixture into twelve mounds.
4. Refrigerate for two hours before serving.

Spinach Dip

Serves: 4
Time: 5 Minutes
Calories: 101 **Protein:** 10 Grams
Fat: 4 Grams **Net Carbs:** 4 Grams
Ingredients:

- 10 Ounces Spinach, Raw
- 1 ½ Cups Greek Yogurt
- 1 Tablespoon Onion Powder
- ½ Teaspoon Garlic Salt
- ½ Teaspoon Greek Seasoning
- Black Pepper to Taste

Directions:

1. Blend everything together, and then seasons to serve.

Cheesy Bacon Sticks

Serves: 4
Time: 15 Minutes
Calories: 278
Protein: 32 Grams
Fat: 15 Grams
Net Carbs: 3 Grams
Ingredients:

- 4 Mozzarella String Cheese Pieces
- 8 Bacon Strips
- Sunflower Oil as Needed

Directions:

1. Start by putting two inches of oil into a skillet, heating it over medium heat.
2. Heat to 350 degrees and halve each string cheese pieces to make eight pieces.
3. Wrap each piece with a strip of bacon, using a toothpick to secure.
4. Cook each one for two minutes until your bacon has browned.
5. Allow to cool before serving.

Green Salmon Bites

Serves: 5
Time: 15 Minutes
Calories: 277
Protein: 19 Grams
Fat: 22 Grams
Net Carbs: 5 Grams
Ingredients:

- 1 Cucumber Sliced in 10 1/3 Inch Rounds
- 1 Avocado, Large
- 8 Ounces Cream Cheese
- 1 Tablespoon Lemon Juice, Fresh
- 4 Ounces Red Salmon Cooked & Flaked
- Tabasco Sauce to Taste
- ½ Tablespoon Green Onion, Chopped

Directions:

1. Halve your avocados, removing the seed before scooping out the flesh.
2. Add your cream cheese to the flesh and lemon juice, mixing well before adding Tabasco sauce.
3. Arrange the cucumber slices on a platter, dividing the avocado mixture on top.
4. Season with red pepper flakes and garnish with green onions before serving.

Dill & Smoked Salmon Spread

Serves: 8
Time: 20 Minutes
Calories: 70
Protein: 5 Grams
Fat: 5 Grams
Net Carbs: 2 Grams
Ingredients:

- 4 Ounces Smoked Salmon
- 4 Ounces Cream Cheese, Room Temperature
- 2 ½ Tablespoons Mayonnaise
- 2 Tablespoons Dill Fresh & Chopped
- Cucumber & Tomato Wedges for Serving
- Sea Salt & Black Pepper to Taste

Directions:

1. Pulse your cream cheese, salmon and mayonnaise in a food processor
2. Add dill. Mix well, and then serve with tomato or cucumber wedges.

Parmesan Crackers

Serves: 8
Time: 15 Minutes
Calories: 133
Protein: 11 Grams
Fat: 11 Grams
Net Carbs: 1 Gram
Ingredients:
- 1 Teaspoon Butter
- 8 Ounces Parmesan Cheese, Full Fat & Shredded

Directions:
1. Start by heating your oven to 400, and then line a baking sheet using parchment paper. Grease with butter.
2. Spoon your cheese into mounds, and then make sure they're flat.
3. Bake until the edges are browned, which should take five minutes.
4. Allow to cool before serving. If you want to make these in advance, just bake them for one to two minutes to crisp after thawing.

Walnut Crusted Goat Cheese

Serves: 4
Time: 10 Minutes
Calories: 304
Protein: 12 Grams
Fat: 28 Grams
Net Carbs: 2 Grams
Ingredients:

- 6 Ounces Walnuts Chopped
- 1 Tablespoon Oregano Chopped
- 1 Tablespoon Parsley Chopped
- ¼ Teaspoon Black Pepper
- 1 Teaspoon Thyme Fresh & Chopped
- 8 Ounces Goat Cheese

Directions:

1. Put your parsley, thyme, walnuts, pepper and oregano into a food processor pulsing until chopped fine.
2. Pour the mixture into a bowl, rolling your goat cheese in it.
3. Store in the fridge for up to a week, slicing to serve.

Pepper & Bacon Bombs

Serves: 12
Time: 1 Hour 10 Minutes
Calories: 89
Protein: 3 Grams
Fat: 8 Grams
Net Carbs: 0 Grams
Ingredients:

- 2 Ounces Goat Cheese, Room Temperature
- 8 Bacon Slices, Cooked & Chopped
- Black Pepper to taste
- 2 Ounces Cream Cheese, Room Temperature
- ¼ Cup Butter, Room Temperature

Directions:

1. Line a baking sheet with parchment paper.
2. Mix your cream cheese, butter, bacon, pepper and goat cheese in a bowl until combined well.
3. Use a tablespoon to drop the bombs onto your baking sheet, allowing it to sit in the freezer for an hour before transferring to the fridge.

Cheesy Bacon Deviled Eggs

Serves: 12
Time: 15 Minutes
Calories: 85 **Protein:** 6 Grams
Fat: 7 Grams **Net Carbs:** 2 Grams
Ingredients:
- 6 Hardboiled Eggs, Peeled
- ¼ Cup Creamy Mayonnaise
- ¼ Avocado, Chopped
- ¼ Cup Swiss Cheese, Shredded Fine
- ½ Teaspoon Dijon Mustard
- 6 Bacon Slices, Cooked & Chopped
- Black Pepper to Taste

Directions:
1. Halve all your eggs lengthwise, and then remove the yolks placing them into a bowl.
2. Put your whites on a plate.
3. Mash your yolks, adding cheese, avocado, Dijon mustard and mayonnaise, mixing well. Season with black pepper before spooning the mixture back into your egg whites to serve.

Dinner Recipes

Dinner can be difficult to cook when you've just gotten home from a day out or just a long day at work, which is why meal prepping is so important.

Ginger Soup

Serves: 4
Time: 20 Minutes
Calories: 65
Protein: 7 Grams
Fat: 2 Grams
Net Carbs: 5 Grams
Ingredients:
- 1 Can Diced Tomatoes
- 1 Can Peppers
- 6 Cups Vegetable Broth
- 3 Cups Green Onions, Diced
- 2 Cups Mushrooms, Sliced
- 3 Teaspoons Garlic, minced
- 3 Teaspoons Ginger, Fresh & Grated
- 4 Tablespoons Tamari
- 2 Cups Bok Choy, Chopped
- 1 Tablespoon Cilantro, Chopped

- 3 Tablespoons Carrot Grated

Directions:
1. Add all ingredients except for your carrot and green onion into a saucepan, and then bring it to a boil using medium-high heat.
2. Lower to medium-low, cooking for six minutes.
3. Stir in your carrots and green onions, cooking for another two minutes.
4. Serve with cilantro.

Fish Taco Bowls

Serves: 4
Time: 25 Minutes
Calories: 315 **Protein:** 16 Grams
Fat: 24 Grams **Net Carbs:** 5 Grams
Ingredients:

- 4 Tilapia Fillets, 5 Ounces Each
- 8 Teaspoons Tajin Seasoning Salt, Divided
- 2 Tablespoons Olive Oil
- 4 Cups Coleslaw Cabbage Mix
- 2 Tablespoons Red Pepper Miso Mayonnaise + Some for Serving
- 2 Avocados, Mashed
- Sea Salt & Black Pepper to Taste

Directions:

1. Start by heating your oven to 425, lining a baking sheet with foil.
2. Rub your tilapia down with olive oil, and seasoning it.
3. Bake for fifteen minutes, and then allow it to cool.
4. In a bowl, combine your mayonnaise and coleslaw, and top with fish to serve. Add in your mashed avocado.

Scallops in Bacon Sauce

Serves: 4
Time: 25 Minutes
Calories: 728
Protein: 24 Grams
Fat: 73 Grams
Net Carbs: 10 Grams
Ingredients:
- 2 Cups Heavy Whipping Cream
- 2 Tablespoons Butter
- 8 Bacon Slices
- ½ Cup Parmesan Cheese, Grated
- 2 Tablespoons Ghee
- 16 Scallops, Large & Patted Dry
- Sea Salt & Black Pepper to Taste

Directions:
1. Place a skillet over medium-high heat, and then cook your bacon. It should take eight minutes.

2. Lower the heat to medium, then add in parmesan cheese, butter and cream. Season with salt and pepper, and then reduce to low. Cook,

stirring constantly. It should thicken and reduce by half in ten minutes.

3. Put another skillet over medium-high heat, heating until your ghee begins to sizzle.

4. Season your scallops with salt and pepper, adding them to the skillet. Cook for a minute per side. Make sure you don't crowd your scallops.

5. Serve with your cream sauce with crumbled bacon on top.

Buttery Garlic Shrimp

Serves: 4
Time: 25 Minutes
Calories: 329 **Protein:** 32 Grams
Fat: 20 Grams **Net Carbs:** 4 Grams
Ingredients:

- 6 Tablespoons Butter
- 1 lb. Shrimp, Cooked
- 2 Lemons, Halved
- ½ Teaspoon Red Pepper Flakes
- 4 Cloves Garlic, Crushed
- Sea Salt & Black Pepper to Taste

Directions:

1. Start by heating your oven to 425, and then place your butter in an eight-inch baking dish. The butter should melt.
2. Sprinkle your shrimp with salt and pepper, and then slice your lemon halves into thin slices.
3. Add your shrimp, garlic and butter into your baking dish. Sprinkle with red pepper flakes, cooking for fifteen minutes. Stir halfway through, and then squeeze the lemon wedges across the dish before serving.

Cheesy Salmon & Asparagus

Serves: 4
Time: 30 Minutes
Calories: 434 **Protein:** 42 Grams
Fat: 26 Grams **Net Carbs:** 6 Grams
Ingredients:

- 4 Salmon Fillets, 6 Ounces Each & Skin On
- 2 lbs. Asparagus, Trimmed
- 6 Tablespoons Butter
- 4 Cloves Garlic, Minced
- ½ Cup Parmesan Cheese, Grated
- Sea Salt & Black Pepper to Taste

Directions:

1. Start by heating your oven to 400, lining a baking sheet with foil.
2. Pat your salmon dry, seasoning with salt and pepper.
3. Put your salmon in a pan, arranging your asparagus around it.
4. Put a saucepan over medium heat and melt your butter. Add in your garlic, stirring until it browns which takes about three minutes. Drizzle this butter over your salmon and asparagus.
5. Top with parmesan cheese and then cook for twelve minutes. Broil for another three before serving warm.

Herb Pork Chops

Serves: 4
Time: 30 Minutes
Calories: 333 **Protein:** 31 Grams
Fat: 23 Grams **Net Carbs:** 0 Grams
Ingredients:

- 2 Tablespoons Butter + More for Coating
- 4 Pork Chops, Boneless
- 2 Tablespoons Italian Seasoning
- 2 Tablespoons Italian Leaf Parsley Chopped
- 2 Tablespoons Olive Oil
- Sea Salt & Black Pepper to Taste

Directions:

1. Start by heating your oven to 350 and coat a baking dish with butter.
2. Season your pork chops, and then top with fresh parsley, drizzling with olive oil and a half a tablespoon of butter each to bake.
3. Bake for twenty to twenty-five minutes.

Paprika Chicken

Serves: 4
Time: 35 Minutes
Calories: 389 **Protein:** 25 Grams
Fat: 30 Grams **Net Carbs:** 4 Grams
Ingredients:

- 2 Teaspoons Smoked Paprika
- ½ Cup Heavy Whipping Cream
- ½ Cup Sweet Onion, Chopped
- 1 Tablespoon Olive Oil
- 4 Chicken Breasts, Skin On & 4 Ounces Each
- ½ Cup Sour Cream
- 2 Tablespoons Parsley, Chopped

Directions:

1. Season your chicken with salt and pepper, putting a skillet over medium-high heat. Add your oil, and once it simmers, sear your chicken on both sides. It should take about fifteen minutes to cook your chicken all the way through. Put your chicken to the side.
2. Add in your onion, sautéing for four minutes or until tender.
3. Stir in your paprika and cream, bringing it to a simmer.
4. Return your chicken to the skillet, simmering for five more minutes.
5. Stir in sour cream and serve topped with parsley.

Coconut Chicken

Serves: 4 **Time:** 40 Minutes
Calories: 382
Protein: 23 Grams **Fat:** 31 Grams **Net Carbs:** 4 Grams
Ingredients:

- 1 Teaspoon Ground Cumin
- 1 Teaspoon Ground Coriander
- ¼ Cup Cilantro, Fresh & Chopped
- 1 Cup Coconut Milk
- 1 Tablespoon Curry Powder
- ½ Cup Sweet Onion, Chopped
- 2 Tablespoons Olive Oil
- 4 Chicken Breasts, 4 Ounces Each & Cut into 2 Inch Chunks

Directions:

1. Get out a saucepan, adding in your oil and heating it over medium-high heat.

2. Sauté your chicken until it's almost completely cooked, which will take roughly ten minutes.

3. Add in your onion, cooking for another three minutes.

4. Whisk your curry powder, coconut milk, coriander and cumin together.

5. Pour the sauce into your pan, bringing it to a boil with your chicken.

6. Reduce the heat, and let it simmer for ten minutes.

7. Serve topped with cilantro.

Taco Casserole

Serves: 8 **Time:** 1 Hour 30 Minutes
Calories: 242 **Protein:** 18 Grams
Fat: 17 Grams **Net Carbs:** 4 Grams
Ingredients:

- 1 lb. Ground Turkey
- 1 Cauliflower, Small & Chopped into Florets
- 1 Jalapeno Diced
- ¼ Cup Red Peppers, Diced
- ¼ Cup Onion, Diced
- 1 Teaspoon Cumin
- 1 Teaspoon Parsley
- 1 Teaspoon Garlic Minced
- 1 Teaspoon Turmeric
- 1 Teaspoon Oregano
- 1 ½ Cups Cheddar Cheese, Shredded
- 1 Cup Sour Cream

Directions:

1. Put your minced meat and cauliflower in a bowl before adding all your herbs and spices. Stir in your red peppers, jalapenos and onions together, mixing in a cup of your cheese.
2. Pour into a casserole dish before topping with remaining cheese.
3. Bake at 350 for an hour and serve with sour cream.

Cabbage & Chicken Plates

Serves: 4
Time: 25 Minutes
Calories: 368
Protein: 42 Grams
Fat: 18 Grams
Net Carbs: 8 Grams

Ingredients:
- 1 Cup Bean Sprouts, Fresh
- 2 Tablespoons Sesame & Garlic Flavored Oil
- ½ Cup Onion, Sliced
- 4 Cups Bok Choy, Shredded
- 3 Stalks Celery, Chopped
- 1 Tablespoon Ginger, Minced
- 2 Tablespoon Coconut Aminos
- 1 Teaspoon Stevia
- 1 Cup Chicken Broth
- 1 ½ Teaspoons Minced Garlic
- 1 Teaspoon Arrowroot

- 4 Chicken Breasts, Boneless, Cooked & Sliced Thin

Directions:

1. Shred your cabbage, and then add your chicken and onion together.
2. Add in a dollop of mayonnaise if desired, drizzling with oil
3. Season as desired and serve.

Grilled Chicken & Cheesy Spinach

Serves: 6
Time: 15 Minutes
Calories: 195
Protein: 30 Grams
Fat: 7 Grams
Net Carbs: 3 Grams
Ingredients:
- 3 Ounces Mozzarella Cheese, Part Skim
- 3 Chicken Breasts, Large & Sliced in Half
- 10 Ounces Spinach, Frozen, Thawed & Drained
- ½ Cup Roasted Red Peppers, Sliced into Strips
- 2 Cloves Garlic Minced
- 1 Teaspoon Olive Oil
- Sea Salt & Black Pepper to Taste

Directions:
1. Start by heating your oven to 400, and then grease a pan.
2. Bake your chicken breasts for two to three minutes per side.
3. In another skillet, cook your garlic and spinach in oil for three minutes.
4. Put your chicken on a pan, topping it with spinach, roasted peppers and mozzarella.
5. Bake until your cheese melts and serve warm.

Balsamic Chicken with Vegetables

Serves: 4 **Time:** 40 Minutes
Calories: 248 **Protein:** 27 Grams
Fat: 8 Grams **Net Carbs:** 14 Grams
Ingredients:

- 8 chicken Cutlets, Skinless & Boneless
- ½ Cup Buttermilk, Low Fat
- 4 Tablespoons Dijon Mustard
- 2/3 Cup Almond Meal
- 2/3 Cup Cashews Chopped
- 4 Teaspoons Stevia
- ¾ Teaspoon Rosemary
- Sea Salt & Black Pepper to Taste

Directions:

1. Start by heating your oven to 425.
2. Mix your buttermilk and mustard together in a bowl
3. Add your chicken, coating it.
4. Put a skillet over medium heat, and then add in your almond meal. Bake until its golden, putting it in a bowl.
5. Add your sea salt, pepper, rosemary and cashews, mixing well. Coat your chicken with the almond meal mix, and then put it in a baking pan.
6. Bake for twenty-five minutes.

Steak & Broccoli Medley

Serves: 4
Time: 20 Minutes
Calories: 875 **Protein:** 40 Grams
Fat: 75 Grams **Net Carbs:** 10 Grams
Ingredients:

- 4 Ounces Butter
- ¾ lb. Ribeye Steak
- 9 Ounces Broccoli
- 1 Yellow Onion
- 1 Tablespoon Coconut Aminos
- 1 Tablespoon Pumpkin Seeds
- Sea Salt & Black Pepper as Needed

Directions:

1. Slice your onion and steak before chopping your broccoli.
2. Put a frying pan over medium heat, adding in butter. Let it melt, and then add meat. Season with salt and pepper, placing your meat to the side.
3. Brown your onion and broccoli, adding more butter as necessary.
4. Add in your coconut aminos before adding your meat back.
5. Serve topped with pumpkin seeds and butter.

Stuffed Meat Loaf

Serves: 8 **Time:** 1 Hour 20 Minutes
Calories: 248 **Protein:** 15 Grams
Fat: 20 Grams **Net Carbs:** 1 Gram
Ingredients:
- 17 Ounces Ground Beef
- ¼ Cup Onions, Diced
- 6 Slices Cheddar Cheese
- ¼ Cup Green Onions, Diced
- ½ Cup Spinach
- ¼ Cup Mushrooms

Directions:
1. Mix your salt, pepper, meat, cumin and garlic together before greasing a pan.
2. Put your cheese on the bottom of your meatloaf, adding in the spinach, mushrooms and onions, and then use leftover meat to cover the top.
3. Bake at 350 for an hour before serving.

Beef Cabbage Rolls

Time: 6 Hours 15 Minutes
Serves: 5
Calories: 481
Protein: 35 Grams
Fat: 25 Grams
Net Carbs: 4 Grams
Ingredients:

- 3 ½ lb. Corned Beef
- 15 Cabbage Leaves, Large
- 1 Onion
- 1 Lemon
- ¼ Cup Coffee
- ¼ Cup White Wine
- 1 Tablespoon Bacon Fat, Rendered
- 1 Tablespoon Brown Mustard
- 2 Tablespoons Himalayan Pink Sea Salt
- 2 Tablespoons Worcestershire Sauce
- 1 Teaspoon Whole Peppercorns
- 1 Teaspoon Mustard Seeds
- ½ Teaspoon Red Pepper Flakes
- ¼ Teaspoons Cloves
- ¼ Teaspoon Allspice
- 1 Bay Leaf, Large

Directions:

1. Add your liquids, corned beef and spices into a slow cooker, cooking on low for six hours.

2. Bring a pot of water to a boil, adding your cabbage leaves and one sliced onion, bringing it to a boil for three minutes.

3. Remove your cabbage, putting it in ice water for three to four minutes, continuing to boil your onion.

4. Dry the leaves off, slicing your meat, and adding in your cooked onion and meat into your leaves.

Side Dish Recipes

No dinner would be complete without a proper side dish, so here are some recipes to help!

Garlic Artichokes

Serves: 6
Time: 35 Minutes
Calories: 237
Protein: 5 Grams
Fat: 19 Grams
Net Carbs: 12 Grams
Ingredients:

- 2 Artichokes, Large
- 1 Lemon Quartered
- ¾ Cup Olive Oil
- 4 Garlic Cloves Chopped
- 1 Teaspoon Sea Salt, Fine
- ½ Teaspoon Black Pepper

Directions:

1. Add water to a large bowl, squeezing your lemon into it.
2. Trim the tops from your artichokes before halving them lengthwise.
3. Bring your water to a boil, adding in your artichokes, letting them cook for fifteen minutes.
4. Preheat your grill to a medium-high, and then drain your artichokes once they're cooked. Squeeze the rest of the juice from your lemon wedges. Stir in your olive oil and garlic, seasoning with salt and pepper.
5. Brush your artichokes with the garlic dip, putting them on a pre-heated grill. Grill for ten minutes, and then serve.

Creamed Spinach

Serves: 4
Time: 40 Minutes
Calories: 195 **Protein:** 3 Grams
Fat: 20 Grams **Net Carbs:** 1 Gram
Ingredients:

- 1 Tablespoon Butter
- ½ Sweet Onion, Sliced Thin
- 4 Cups Spinach, Stemmed & Washed
- ¾ Cup Heavy Whipping Cream
- ¼ Cup Herbed Chicken Stock
- 1 Pinch Ground Nutmeg
- Sea Salt & Black Pepper to Taste

Directions:

1. Get out a skillet, placing it over medium heat with your butter in it.
2. Sauté your onion for five minutes or until caramelized.
3. Stir in the heavy cream, chicken stock, spinach, nutmeg, salt and pepper, sautéing for five minutes. Your spinach should wilt.
4. Continue to cook your spinach until tender and the sauce thickens. It should take fifteen minutes.

Onion Rings

Serves: 4
Time: 25 Minutes
Calories: 323 **Protein:** 15 Grams
Fat: 26 Grams **Net Carbs:** 5 Grams
Ingredients:

- 8 Tablespoons Parmesan Cheese Grated
- 1 Teaspoon Garlic Powder
- A Dash Sea Sat
- 1 Tablespoon Olive Oil
- Black Pepper to Taste
- 1 Egg
- 1 Onion, Large
- 1 Cup Almond Flour

Directions:

1. Heat your oven to 400 degrees, and peel and slice your onions into rings that are an inch thick.
2. Combine all dry ingredients into a bowl, mixing well.
3. Whisk your eggs in a different bowl, preparing a baking sheet with parchment paper. Dip your onion rings into the egg and then coat them in the dry mixture, laying them on the baking sheet.
4. Drizzle with olive oil and bake for twenty minutes. They should be crisp and golden.

Cheesy Mashed Cauliflower

Serves: 4
Time: 20 Minutes
Calories: 183 **Protein:** 8 Grams
Fat: 15 Grams **Net Carbs:** 4 Grams
Ingredients:

- 1 Head Cauliflower Chopped
- ½ Cup Cheddar Cheese, Shredded
- 2 Tablespoons Butter, Room Temperature
- ¼ Cup Heavy Whipping Cream
- Sea Salt & Black Pepper to Taste

Directions:

1. Fill a large saucepan with water until its three quarters full. Bring it to a boil over high heat, blanching your cauliflower until tender. This should take about five minutes, and then drain your cauliflower.

2. Place your cauliflower in a food processor, adding in all other ingredients until creamy.

Mushrooms & Camembert

Serves: 4
Time: 20 Minutes
Calories: 161
Protein: 9 Grams
Fat: 13 Grams
Net Carbs: 3 Grams
Ingredients:

- 2 Tablespoons Butter
- 1 lb. Button Mushrooms Halved
- 2 Teaspoons Garlic Minced
- 4 Ounces Camembert Cheese Diced
- Black Pepper to Taste

Directions:

1. Put a skillet over medium-high heat to melt your butter, adding in your garlic to sauté for three minutes.
2. Sauté your mushrooms until tender, which should take about ten minutes.
3. Add in your cheese, sautéing until melted, which should take about two minutes.
4. Season with pepper before serving.

Roasted Radishes

Serves: 4
Time: 25 Minutes
Calories: 181 **Protein:** 1 Gram
Fat: 19 Grams **Net Carbs:** 2 Grams
Ingredients:

- 4 Cups Radishes Halved
- 2 Tablespoons Olive Oil
- 4 Tablespoons Butter
- 2 Tablespoons Italian Parsley
- Sea Salt & Black Pepper to Taste

Directions:

1. Heat your oven to 450, and then get out a bowl.

2. Toss your radishes in olive oil, seasoning with salt and pepper.

3. Spread your radishes out on a baking sheet in a single layer, allowing them to roast for fifteen minutes. Stir halfway through.

4. Place a saucepan over medium heat, melting your butter and stir frequently to keep them from burning. Season with salt, and then continue to stir as it foams.

5. Serve your radishes with the browned butter.

Parmesan Pork Green Beans

Serves: 4
Time: 20 Minutes
Calories: 175 **Protein:** 6 Grams
Fat: 15 Grams **Net Carbs:** 5 Grams
Ingredients:
- 2 Tablespoons Parmesan Cheese
- Sea Salt & Black Pepper to Taste
- ½ lb. Pork Rinds, Crushed
- 2 Tablespoons Olive Oil

Directions:
1. Start by heating your oven to 400, and then combine your green beans, pork rinds, cheese and olive oil in a bowl. Season with salt and pepper, tossing to coat.
2. Spread your bean mixture on a baking sheet, roasting for fifteen minutes. Turn halfway through and serve warm.

Roasted Brussels Sprouts

Serves: 4
Time: 30 Minutes
Calories: 248
Protein: 14 Grams
Fat: 18 Grams
Net Carbs: 7 Grams
Ingredients:

- 1 lb. Brussels Sprouts Trimmed
- 2 Tablespoons Olive Oil
- 2 Teaspoons Red Pepper Flakes
- 12 Slices Bacon
- 2 Tablespoons Parmesan Cheese Grated
- Sea Salt & Black Pepper to Taste

Directions:

1. Start by heating your oven to 400.
2. Toss your Brussels sprouts in olive oil, red pepper flakes, sea salt and pepper.
3. Chop your bacon into one-inch pieces.
4. Put your bacon and Brussels sprouts on a baking sheet, roasting for twenty-five minutes. Shake it halfway through.
5. Serve with parmesan cheese.

Sautéed Zucchini

Serves: 6
Time: 35 Minutes
Calories: 230
Protein: 5 Grams
Fat: 22 Grams
Net Carbs: 4 Grams
Ingredients:

- 4 Zucchini, Halved & Sliced
- ½ Red Onion, Diced
- 1 Tablespoon Olive Oil
- ½ lb. Mushrooms, Sliced
- 1 Tomato Diced
- 1 Garlic Cloves Minced
- 1 Teaspoons Italian Seasoning

Directions:

1. Place a skillet over medium heat, and then add in your onions. Cook for two minutes, seasoning with salt and pepper.
2. Add zucchini, cooking until tender.
3. Season with garlic and Italian seasoning before serving.

Dessert Recipes

Dessert may not be an important meal of the day, but many people love to indulge. Here are some dessert recipes that you can cook in advance and enjoy whenever you want.

Raspberry Scones

Serves: 12
Time: 25 Minutes
Calories: 133
Protein: 2 Grams
Fat: 8 Grams
Net Carbs: 4 Grams
Ingredients:

- 3 Eggs, Beaten
- 1 ½ Cups Almond Flour
- ¾ Cup Raspberries, Fresh
- ½ Cup Stevia
- 2 Teaspoons Vanilla Extract, Pure
- 2 Teaspoons Baking Powder

Directions:
1. Start by preheating your oven to 375, and then line a baking sheet with parchment paper.
2. Take a bowl, mixing your stevia, vanilla, eggs, almond flour and baking powder together, whisking well.
3. Fold your raspberries in and create mounds with the batter on your baking sheet.
4. Bake for fifteen minutes before allowing cooling.

Coconut Macaroons

Serves: 18
Time: 2 Hours 20 Minutes
Calories: 47 **Protein:** 0.4 Grams
Fat: 5 Grams **Net Carbs:** 2 Grams
Ingredients:

- 1 ½ Cups Coconut, Shredded & Unsweetened
- ¾ Cup Coconut Milk, Full Fat
- 2 ¼ Teaspoons Stevia

Directions:

1. Mix all ingredients together, and tightly cover using plastic wrap.

2. Leave in the fridge for two hours before scooping into balls to serve.

Banana Fat Bombs

Serves: 12
Time: 1 Hour 10 Minutes
Calories: 134 **Protein:** 3 Grams
Fat: 12 Grams **Net Carbs:** 1 Gram
Ingredients:
- 1 ¼ Cups Cream Cheese, Room Temperature
- 1 Tablespoon Banana Extract
- 6 Drops Liquid Stevia
- ¾ Cup Heavy Whipping Cream

Directions:
1. Line a baking sheet using parchment paper.

2. Beat your heavy cream, cream cheese, stevia and banana extract until smooth and thick. This should take roughly five minutes.

3. Put mounds of the batter onto the baking sheet, freezing for an hour before serving.

Blueberry Fat Bombs

Serves: 12
Time: 3 Hours 10 Minutes
Calories: 115 **Protein:** 1 Gram
Fat: 12 Grams **Net Carbs:** 1 Gram
Ingredients:

- ½ Cup Coconut Oil, Room Temperature
- 6 Drops Liquid Stevia
- ½ Cup Blueberries, Mashed
- Pinch Nutmeg
- ½ Cup Cream Cheese, Room Temperature

Directions:

1. Get out a mini muffin tin and line it with paper liners, and then get out a bowl.
2. Stir together your coconut oil and cream cheese until blended.
3. Add in your nutmeg, stevia and blueberries, blending well.
4. Divide between your muffin tins and freeze for three hours before serving.

Almond Butter Fudge

Serves: 36
Time: 2 Hours 10 Minutes
Calories: 204 **Protein:** 3 Grams
Fat: 22 Grams **Net Carbs:** 2 Grams
Ingredients:

- 1 Cup Coconut Oil, Room Temperature
- 1 Cup Almond Butter
- 10 Drops Liquid Stevia
- ¼ Cup Heavy Whipping Cream
- Pinch Sea Salt

Directions:

1. Line a six by six-inch pan using parchment paper.

2. Get out a medium bowl, whisking your almond butter, heavy cream, coconut oil, stevia and salt until smooth.

3. Spoon this mixture into a baking dish and refrigerate for two hours before slicing to serve.

Vanilla Popsicles

Serves: 8
Time: 4 Hours 15 Minutes
Calories: 166 **Protein:** 3 Grams
Fat: 15 Grams **Net Carbs:** 2 Grams
Ingredients:

- 1 Cup Coconut, Shredded & Unsweetened
- 2 Cups Almond Milk
- 1 Cup Heavy Whipping Cream
- 1 Vanilla Bean, Halved Lengthwise

Directions:

1. Get out a saucepan, heating it over medium heat. Add together your vanilla bean, heavy cream and almond milk.

2. Bring it all to a simmer, reducing to low heat. Let it simmer for five minutes, and then let it cool.

3. Take out your vanilla bean, and then scrape the seeds out and back into the mixture.

4. Divide between molds after stirring, allowing it to freeze for four hours before serving.

Coffee Popsicles

Serves: 4
Time: 2 Hours 5 Minutes
Calories: 105 **Protein:** 1 Gram
Fat: 10 Grams **Net Carbs:** 2 Grams
Ingredients:

- 2 Cups Coffee, Cold
- ¾ Cup Coconut Cream
- 2 Teaspoons Swerve
- 2 Tablespoons Sugar Free Chocolate Chips

Directions:

1. Start by blending all ingredients together, and then pour into Popsicle molds.

2. Freeze for two hours before serving.

Strawberry Shakes

Serves: 4
Time: 10 Minutes
Calories: 407
Protein: 4 Grams
Fat: 42 Grams
Net Carbs: 6 Grams
Ingredients:

- 1 ½ Cups Heavy Whipping Cream
- 4 Ounces Cream Cheese, Room Temperature
- 2 Tablespoons Swerve
- ½ Teaspoon Vanilla Extract
- 12 Strawberries Fresh & Sliced
- 12 Ice Cubes

Directions:

1. Blend all ingredients together, and then pour into glasses to serve. Chilling your glasses beforehand will make the shakes last even longer!

Raspberry Popsicles

Serves: 4
Time: 2 Hours
Calories: 65 **Protein:** 3 Grams
Fat: 1 Gram **Net Carbs:** 8 Grams
Ingredients:

- ¼ Cup Sour Cream
- ¼ Cup Heavy Cream
- ½ Teaspoon Guar Gum
- 3 ½ Ounces Raspberries
- ½ Lemon, Juiced
- 1 Cup Coconut Milk
- ¼ Cup Coconut Oil
- 20 Drops Liquid Stevia

Directions:

1. Toss all ingredients in a blender and then push through a mesh strainer, discarding the raspberry seeds.

2. Pour the mixture into a mold, allowing it to set in the freezer for about two hours before serving.

Chocolate Bacon

Serves: 6
Time: 35 Minutes
Calories: 258 **Protein:** 7 Grams
Fat: 26 Grams **Net Carbs:** 0.5 Grams
Ingredients:
- 2 ¼ Tablespoons Coconut Oil
- 1 ½ Teaspoons Liquid Stevia
- 4 ½ Tablespoons Dark Chocolate, Unsweetened
- 12 Slices Bacon

Directions:
1. Start by heating your oven to 425, and then skewer your bacon using iron skewers. Arrange your bacon on a baking sheet.
2. Bake until crispy, which should take fifteen minutes.
3. Allow it to cool, getting out a saucepan, putting it over low heat. Melt your coconut oil before stirring in your chocolate.
4. Add in stevia, stirring again.
5. Coat your bacon in the mixture, letting it harden and dry before serving.

Vanilla Pudding

Serves: 4
Time: 20 Minutes
Calories: 135
Protein: 2 Grams
Fat: 13 Grams
Net Carbs: 2 Grams
Ingredients:

- Sea Salt as Needed
- 2 Egg Yolks, Large
- 1 Cup Heavy Cream, 36%
- 1 ½ Teaspoons Stevia
- 1 Teaspoon Arrowroot Flour
- ½ Teaspoon Vanilla Extract, Pure

Directions:

1. Get out a heavy-duty saucepan, adding in egg yolks and whisking in the arrowroot flour, cream, vanilla, and stevia together.
2. Season with salt and whisk again.
3. Put over medium heat, stirring until it begins to steam.
4. Lower the heat, continuing to stir for ten minutes.
5. Pour into four containers to cool before serving.

Poppy Seed Cupcakes

Serves: 4
Time: 35 Minutes
Calories: 229 **Protein:** 6 Grams
Fat: 15 Grams **Net Carbs:** 14 Grams
Ingredients:

- ¾ Cup Blanched Almond Flour
- 1/3 Cup Erythritol
- ¼ Cup Golden Flaxseed Meal
- 2 Tablespoons Poppy Seeds
- 1 Teaspoon Baking Powder
- 3 Eggs, Large
- ¼ Cup Salted Butter, Liquid
- ¼ Cup Heavy Cream
- 2 Lemons, Zested
- 3 Tablespoons Lemon Juice, Fresh
- 25 Drops Liquid Stevia
- 1 Teaspoon Vanilla Extract

Directions:

1. Start by heating your oven to 350, and then get out a bowl.
2. Mix your Erythritol, almond flour and poppy seeds, adding in your flaxseed meal stir in melted butter and heavy cream, and then add in your egg. Mix well, pouring into cupcake molds.
3. Bake for twenty minutes, letting cool before serving.

Conclusion

Now you know everything you need to get started meal prepping while still sticking to your ketogenic diet.

Remember that meal prepping isn't perfect in the beginning, but the goal is to get where you only must cook once a week and still enjoy healthy meals that delight your taste buds! Just plan your meals accordingly and remember to mark each package with how many net carbs are in a serving so that you stay in ketosis and enjoy all the benefits that the ketogenic diet has to offer.

This this ketogenic meal prep guide can help you to save your time and money!

With the ketogenic diet, you're choosing a lifestyle that's meant to help you reach a healthier, happier you. Like any lifestyle change, it can be a hassle, especially when you're trying to cook three healthy meals a day after a hard day's work.

That's where meal prepping can help. This book will teach you meal prepping recipes you can use for breakfast, lunch, dinner, snacks and even dessert.

Made in the USA
Lexington, KY
09 November 2018